The Way I Felt

A Collection of Poems From My
High School Years

A.C. Ham

The Way I Felt: A Collection of Poems From My High School Years

A.C. Ham © 2021

Bogart, Georgia

abbyhamauthor@gmail.com

Cover picture by Abby Ham.

Dedication

To growth. One never knows how much change they
need until they've achieved it. I've changed so much
since the last poem in here was written, and I still
have so much progress ahead of me. Thanks to these
poems, I'm able to look back at the landmarks of my
emotions and see how much I've grown.

Table of Contents

Promises
Closer and Still
Where You Are
Masterpiece
Lost in Fog
Let Me
Signs of Love

6. <u>To My Friends</u>
The Color Blue/Love
Generation
A Conversation With a Friend
Plague Mask Guy
Galaxy Boy
Summer's Tip
A Joker in a Saint's Skin
Time to Stop
Maybe Best Friend
Senior Year
The Age of Friendships

7. <u>For No One but Myself</u>
A Thought
Take Me to the Gardens
Escape From Reality
In the Meadow
A Poem for Me

Over It

Fleeting Thought

A Message From the Author

When I first began compiling the poems I had (mostly) written in my senior year of high school, I decided to name this book *The Way I Feel*. As you can see from the cover, the name has been slightly altered.

As I began to type up some of the poems (particularly those in chapters 3, 13, and 14), I realized that I have different feelings about the situations I had previously written about. Growth is always a tricky subject. I mean, you can always backtrack your own progress accidentally, and for me, growth in how I handled my emotions was something I'd been waiting for. When I realized how I've been able to let go of the hurt, anger, infatuation, and loneliness I'd been unknowingly holding onto, I felt ... relieved.

So take all these poems with a grain of salt, knowing that (most of) the things I wrote about are in the past. I am no longer hurt or angry, the wounds I wrote of are now healed, and I'm able to release this book from a better place, knowing whatever I write next will need just as much growth as this book did.

Introduction

In this book, I hope you find a poem for yourself.
This book, I hope, won't collect dust on a shelf.

Hopefully, you'll find yourself a flower,
Gentle, kind, and full of power.
Maybe you'll find yourself in my shoes,
Wandering the cornfields, feeling blue.
But possibly, you'll find yourself the villain
In the story you didn't know you ruined.

Whatever the perspective may be,
I hope you'll continue to read.
These poems are for you as well as me.
On ink and paper, we begin our stories
Of old love and newer heartbreak
And in between a million mistakes.
Of places I've been or never will go,
Of things I knew to things I now know.

1. Spring

In The Clover Field

I sit in a patch of clover
In my worn-out overalls.
The terror isn't over.
Justice still calls.

I lie amongst the blooming greens,
Breathe the dewy smell.
I stare at the sky's blue sheen
And know it will all be well.

I turn to find something to pluck
As hair covers my face.
I'm hoping—
no, praying—
for luck
For the entire human race,
But luscious leaves and dewy stems
Can't end the reaper's theft,
So run away with me on this whim.
They'll never know we've left.

Teacher's Blossoms
(this poem uses flower language)2

On my kindergarten teacher's desk were pink carnations.
They're pink and perky, like the voice she speaks in.
I don't remember much of Miss Barnett,
I'm not even sure that's her name,
But when I think of kindergarten, this picture came:
Pink Carnations on a desk,
Nothing more and nothing less.

My mom taught me and still does,
A sweet honeysuckle in full bud.
The guiding hand that nurtures me
Is like the sweet blossoms in hanging ivy:
It's always there and ready to help,
Even if discarded on a creaky shelf.
She's always there whenever I need her.
All these years and she's still a teacher.

She doodles the likes of Acanthus and Angelica,
Not caring what people make of her.
A watchful eye and confidante,
She watches my painted song.
She's the watering can the Gardener uses,
And she herself has many muses.

My English teacher smells of sage,
Same as the advice she gave.
Standing stern and standing strong,

She's nice even when I'm wrong.
She helps with educational growth,
One I didn't like but now favor most.

"Y el flores o mi espaniol professora"
Are Coreopsis, the kind we need more of.
She's a smile in the summer rain,
The first clap at the last refrain.

If I wrote a poem about Pink Rose,
She would read it because she knows.
She guides my computer keys and pencil lead
And helped inspire the words you've read.
She prompted and she poked,
Then my character spoke.

White honeysuckle is she who signs,
Who when I was lost was a willing guide.
Her smile greets the whole classroom,
A ray of sunshine amidst the gloom.

Sweet Basil, mislabeled goldenrod,
Who often asks if the day was bad.
We disagreed, but she helped me know.
I've grown a lot. I still could grow.

The Lightning

Like a light switch poised between on and off,
Lightning strikes, causing the colors to pop.
Like a painting with its colors now changed,
A lightning strike can make the familiar seem strange.

The Storm

Sometimes things just cultivate,
Resulting in a spiraling hate.
Sometimes things get pent up,
Spilling out of a too-full cup.

Emotions can tornado out of control,
Causing more damage than we know.
A perfect storm is bound to occur,
But it leaves reminders of how things were.

If this siren's warning suddenly went off,
What would be gained in the midst of the loss?

So many evacuate in the storm
While others stand by me, becoming well worn.

If you think you could survive,
Risk it all and give it a try.
I'll be here when the grass has dried.

2. G.G.

12/07/20

In the window, there was a bluebird.
It never whistled, never said a word,
Yet when I visited, you pointed it out,
That little clay bird, short, sweet, and stout.
Beneath the bird, an African violet sat,
Its joyful petals spread over its leafy lap.
You pointed it out to those who could see,
Which caused the giver, a third in line, much glee.
Around you were faces from our tree of genetics,
All smiling and posed or laughing and hectic.
Some of the faces were bathed in golden light,
While others were painted in black and white.
The last time I saw you, you sang us a song,
About a moose in some tracks, as you sat in our throng,
But today all the world is silent.
Even our salty tears fall in quiet.
You had told me a story about the white pinecone land,
And how, when you moved here, you missed the sand.
Your dad caught seafood, though you got none.
That food was for selling; it was a treat to get some.
One day there was a record playing in the living room.
It told the story of a boy, someone you once knew.
You would tell a tale, and the whole world listened,
But someone will read this now as their eyelashes
glisten.
We'll have to go up north when the ground's not frozen
And watch amongst the buttonbushes as the ground gets
opened.

Then you'll become a daffodil in the Lord's field,
While here on earth things have yet to yield.
You, a grandmother and a storyteller with heart,
You were a world changer who left a lasting mark.
And when the bluebird sings, I'll see you still
And that little clay bird on the windowsill.

The Funeral's Echo

Roses and sunflowers in a bed with daisies.
A cross made of blue ribbons and lilies.
It's loud when there's laughter;
Without it, it's deafening.

The day goes on, performances pass,
But when the singing ends, there's not a single clap.
The quiet gets quieter;
The laughter is lessening.

Would you have wanted me to cry
Or wanted me to smile fondly?
Would you have stopped to ask me why
I'm sitting here so calmly?

'Cause you asked me questions
Whose answers didn't exist
And you sang me songs
With your own lyrics.

And you told me stories
Of things I didn't know.
So how could I tell you,
Your funeral's an echo?

Stories, memories, all passed around.
An echo chamber filling with sound.
With so few friends,

The pews filled with ghosts.

The night goes on, memories are swapped.
With one more song, all chords stop.
More laughs start,
Welcoming the hosts.

Would you have wanted me to cry
Or wanted me to smile fondly?
Would you ask me why
I'm still smiling calmly?

3. Could've Destroyed Me

The Bathroom Floor

I'm sitting in the bathroom. I needed to breathe.
Nothing from today has brought me peace.
There are some girls here, they're gossiping,
And now my stall is filled with screams.

A part of me really wants to cry,
A more dramatic part wants to die.

One girl had a guy flirt with her;
The other girls want to hear the dirt.
I'm sitting here and I hurt
Because you're out there ... With her.

You two are cute, I admit,
But I think that we could fit.
You're right there in front of me
But you're too blind to ever see.

I'm gonna sit here until it's time
'Cause a boy isn't a good reason to cry.
I'm not gonna listen to all of the lies
Because one day I'm gonna be fine.
Maybe one day you'll be mine.

Now there's a wall against my skin.
I can talk but you won't listen.
I play a game I'll never win,
But a crush is not a sin.

I was mad at my friend today
And now we're going separate ways ...
Maybe I should step away
But I don't know what to say.

And now I'm sitting on my bed,
All these things run through my head.
Maybe next time I'll speak instead.
Could be worse—I could be dead.

Mirror

You're not my mirror; you have a shorter frame.
You're nothing like me ... maybe I'm insane.
You're a nicer image for the world to see,
Yet you have the same name as me.

Even though we both use the same shortened,
One of us has made the name worsen.
Funny thing about our name, you don't know I have it.
So many people do, so I guess the name fits.

But it's impersonal to know the two of us share
A name that's been through so much wear and tear.
If you ever read this ... well, that'll be absurd.
You and I haven't shared a single word.

We have two things in common—two makes us twins.
One is a coincidence; the other makes my head spin.
Either of these things would be believable,
But both at once feels unnatural.

So if you read this poem, I'm sorry in advance.
This isn't a battle, so please don't take a stance.
A name alone isn't a reason to destroy,
But you could kill me for liking your boy.

Watch Me

Arm falls, eyes briefly meet.
Look away. I'm on the tops of my feet.
I'll keep dancing, all eyes on me.

A million thoughts you'll never know.
All of my questions, the answer is no.
My bright smile is just for show.

"I like you and I loved him"[1]
But only one pair made friends.
I'm still afraid our bond will end.

Leg swept and I lean back,
Waiting to turn to black.
My crush is a set fact.

I'll never tell, you'll never see
Through all the steps of my feet,
I watch you; please watch me.

You'll Never Know

I hate it when you show up and take me by surprise.
I hate it when I see you and it gives me butterflies.
It's not just you I see when I close my eyes
But you're the first I think of when I tell my lies.

Don't look me in the eye, please don't say my name,
I don't need reminders that we don't feel the same.
Walk by me in the hall, ignore me in the group,
I won't even notice, it's nothing new.

Don't worry that I've stalked you; I'm not insane.
In fact, my affections were more mundane.
All the little things I noticed, I kept inside my head.
I'll write them out for you, but remember this instead:
I'll move on, I'll forget, so when you know this is you,
Call me, let me know, say you were watching too.
I don't ask for love, I ask for like, so please tell me you
craved
One more laugh, one more smile, another memory to
save.

Am I insane? It may be so,
To write down all I've felt and known.
I wanted friends, yet I feel a lack
Of people who crave me back.

I'm done moping—I hope you're flattered
Of all the things about you I thought mattered.
Here's the truth and nothing less,

This is the end, so please don't stress.

You're so well-liked—you know that, right?
You're the guy that fills other guys with spite.
When we first met, I saw you filled with virtue
And, despite a bumpy road, I believe that's still true.
You sat with the younger ones, a future mentor,
And when it came to worship, you were front and center.
You're smart—you obviously know that— but you're
also nice.
When we last sat and talked, it was the day's highlight.

(It's been a week, but now I'll write this part.
Despite the thoughts, the writing's hard.)
Remember the night we caused the rain?
I never thought of you the same.
You were drenched by the storm
But kept working though you were worn.
Or in my childhood, by the pool,
Everyone was trying to be cool.
Though you weren't sure, you gathered strength,
Drew close your courage, and owned the day.
I don't know why I remember that,
Maybe what I lack, I think you have.
Oh gosh, there's more I have to say
But you won't read this (I hope, I pray).
Your eyes are bright—they seem to speak:
They laugh, they sing, they shout, they weep.
Your smile's inviting me to come talk to you
Though whatever I say doesn't seem to get through ...

I swear it's not a crush *(I repeat in my mind)*
But please keep up with me when you've left this world
behind.
I never said a word. I respected your boundaries,
Forgive me for writing my thoughts down for all to see.

All these thoughts once in my head, things I never
showed.
If you never figure out this is about you, you'll never
know.

4. Summer

Clovers in a Chainlink Fence

We sit in our cages like wingless birds
and live for nothing. Isn't that absurd?
I believe there's something greater than what we see,
Something that created the grass, sky, and sea,
Yet as I sit in my trifolium prison behind a linked fence,
I realize I myself am among the dense.
We as people are wandering in a green field,
Surrounded on all sides by a force that will not yield.
I have a dream that I will soon be free,
That I will be able to find a happy me.
Yet my acquaintances are all content
With staring at an iron fence.
Sprigs of hope stick around us like hopeful suitors,
Yet we do not pick them. They're for the future.
We do not search amongst the growth.
We have too many seeds to sow,
Yet we make a pastime out of throwing bundles
Against the walls of our shrinking bubble.
We give up our dreams to make a picture,
Using images as our own kind of liquor,
But I myself do not see any sense
In throwing clover at a chainlink fence.
For once it is there, it will be stuck,
And in a prison wall lies all your luck.

Golden Hour

The golden hour is gone. The world cools.
Night wraps us in her arms as darkness pools.
In the midst of croaks and crickets,
There's a silent part of the thicket.
Where snores sound throughout a claystone home
And knitted wool stands above loam,
That's where I sit among Night's cloak.
In the middle of her journey, I awoke.

I ask her questions, yet she stays quiet.
I close my eyes and tell her: "don't try it!"
"I won't fall asleep 'cause dawn doesn't make new.
I want to sit here with you and just stew."
However, her silence begins to lull me,
And I soon fall asleep happy.

Maybe evening is a land of possibility,
But for me, I'm too fast asleep to see.

5. Why I Live and Love

Can You?

Can you imagine being nailed to a tree?
To blow in the wind like a simple leaf.
Can you imagine making that your fate?
To hang there in agony and patiently wait.
Would you do something like that for me,
Let yourself ache for all to see?
To have a public death for the greater good,
To hear of a better day coming and believe it could.
Can you give up what you scarcely have?
Would you do it for your mom or dad?
Would you feel your life fade away?
Would you even lift your head to say:
"Have patience, have peace.
Care for those, even the least."

Maybe you can't imagine it,
But that's the throne on which my savior sits.

That's the price He chose to pay
For us to have that better day.

Sunday Morning

Early woken, early risen,
Prayers offered, word given,
Only a hallelujah can express.

News shared, smiles brightened,
Names introduced, excitement heightened,
A place of worship nonetheless.

Story told, hearts broken,
Hearts cold, hope spoken,
We trust in You regardless.

The darkest, the brightest;
In harvest, in crisis:
In You, we rest.

A Prayer

Hosanna, never leave me. Let me never forsake thee
Carry me into the rough night.
Yahweh, I pray to thee, open my eyes to see.
On wings like birds of prey, let me take flight.

When I began to wander, heaven was my hope.
Lord, let joy be all I'll ever know.
When I was crying out into darkness, You showed me
light.
God, give me virtue so I may fight.
I was drowning. I wanted to sink.
Continue showing me how freeing it is to breathe.
Father, I'm lost and cannot find the road.
Comfort me as I carry this load.

In the midst of the shadow, I still see a spark.
No longer will I tell myself I deserve the dark.
My comfort, my anthem I'll repeat is this:
Lord, let me be the one the devil cannot miss.
Let me be the enemy he'll want to attack.
Allow others to pick up their cross, carry it like a flag.
Our victory will be in this one truth:
The promises of God will see us through.

Promises

He does not force; He only guides.
He gives us choice, a sacrifice.
He does not tell us how to act.
He doesn't give us what we lack.
He has plans for our service,
For each of us has a purpose.
He doesn't need us, but He longs
For all His children who've done wrong.
When we do wrong, the Lord weeps,
So in His promises, our hope keeps.

Closer and Still

I don't deserve to live, but by Your will, I do.
The very fact that I'm alive I owe to You.

Lord, don't lose me in the brambles.
Deliver me from the thorns.
I know I'm not the victim.
Bless those I scorn.

God, let me not be in the wrong,
For I've been wronged too.
But let me forgive my enemies
And lean into You.

Where did You go? Why did You leave?
God, You know I'm lost. Grant me a reprieve!
The woods look so dark. I feel so cold
Life once moved slow. Now I'm growing old.

Will my pace be broken with a single stride?
If I'm lying on the ground, what happens to my pride?

Lord, restore my faith, restore me to Your will,
Bring me closer, and hold me still.

Where You Are

You weren't in the eyes that judged my flaws.
I don't see You when justice calls.
I found You when a stranger said hello.
I saw You in the debate with no bellow.

You didn't call for Your people to fight.
You call us to do what's right.
You said to love others as we love ourselves.
You call us to love others even when we aren't well.
Lord, call us together when we don't agree.
Please open our eyes so we can see.
See that they hurt just as much,
And they still deserve Your love.

You loved the girl uncomfortable in her skin,
Comforted the champion who didn't win,
You loved the woman who deserved the stone.
Help me to love with Your gentle tone.

Masterpiece

Lord, in my darkest moment, You never left my side.
Restore me to Your will; humble my bruised pride.
Lord, let me be a canvas that others can make beautiful.
Let them make something great with what I think is
horrible.
Reform me to Your will.
Lord, hold me still.
Let this moment go in history.
Lord, please use me.
Let me be the one the devil fears.
Let me work through my tears.

Lost In Fog

One day I woke up and realized I couldn't see.
Even then, You were searching for me.
I was lost in a thick fog and couldn't find the road;
You still offered to carry my load.
But even when I'm not thinking of you,
Between hidden crosses and church pews,
You're waiting through the mist.
You're here in the midst
Of my anxieties, stress, and heartbreak.
You love me no matter my state.
I look up and can't see the road ahead,
But You hold my reins and turn my head.
Guide me, oh Lord, tell me your will,
For You have led me and lead me still.
You won't abandon me in the fog or leave me in the
street;
You have places to take me and people for me to meet.
So though the fog obstructs my view,
I'll wait patiently and hold on to You.

Let Me

God, You have been there, even when I was blind.
You promised You wouldn't leave me behind.

You said, "love others as you love yourselves,"
And "continue to love when you feel unwell."

Lord, bring us together when we don't agree.
Open our eyes, help us to see
That they hurt just as much,
And they also need Your touch.

Teach me to love despite feeling wronged.
Let me dedicate my life to your song.

I saw you in the one who would listen;
God, help me see You again.

Signs of Love

Rated superior at the National Fine Arts Festival (Orlando 2021)

In the midst of a fennel maze, I take my stand.
I cry out, "God, where are you, I need your loving hand."
But no voice cries back, no hand reaches out
So in the middle of a maze, I begin to doubt.
I round every bend, each void of a cornerstone.
Even among these friends, I feel so alone.
I begin to wonder, "do I even have a soul?"
And then begin to spiral down a rabbit hole.
What if I'm lost forever, never to be His?
What if I'm left alone and this is all there is?
Suddenly, in my misery, I begin to see
All of the little signs God left for me.
I climb out of the rut and stare up at a hill
That will take me out of here, if according to His will.
There are more signs of love all around me now,
And as I look back, I see more somehow.
In the girl who's been there for me since middle school,
In the boy who stuck up for me by the pool,
By the girl who always has a wave and a smile,
And the adult who knew I needed to talk for a while.
That's where I found God and where I put my hope.
He's the one waiting at the top of this slope.

6. To My Friends

The Color Blue/Love

The cover of the brightest day,
The same hue as the tears she was crying.
Against the norm, her heart belongs with mine.

The color of the ocean's steady sway,
It fills her lungs, but she comes up breathing.
I need you here till the end of the line.

The way his eyes shine when he's feeling gay,
And the cold of winter against his heart's beating.
Against the norm, his heart belongs with mine.

That feeling of cold when you can't find the way,
That desperate search for meaning.
I need you here till the end of the line.

So believe me whenever I say:
Against the norm, your heart belongs with mine.
I need you here till the end of the line.

Generation

I'm lost. I know people lost like me,
People drowning in sadness and apathy.
We're pulled apart, scissors cutting string;
We feel of no use, bells that cannot ring.

We want to escape, yearn to soar,
But we don't realize we'll be on the ocean floor.
We are not Hercules; we are truly lost.
We may fall alongside the likes of Icarus.

We may stumble along the road,
Fall down the rabbit hole,
But how long will it take to return home?
And will our sister still be reading her tome?

If we're chained to a rock, we'll be beaten away,
But either we will wait for a savior or ourselves we save.
Do we seek revenge on the one who chained us?
Or shall we caution others under his lust?

In the end, too many choose to leave,
While others struggle in the deep.
Yes, I am lost, among others like me.

A Conversation With a Friend

You're telling me you're still in love with her
As we're sitting on my kitchen floor.
You think she should be your girl,
That she could be your whole world.
But you follow them like a stray dog;
You're just another thing they analog.
You're not their favorite, not their least.
You're just another stray on the street.
So keep telling me all your wishes,
Piling onto my dirty dishes.
Asking me, "when will the pain end?"
I don't know, but you've just lost a friend.

Plague Mask Guy

For Bones.

Plague Mask Guy. Plague Mask Guy.
The one who makes small children cry.
Don't try to look him in the eye.
He'll scream at you, "the end is nigh."

The two of us were in my car,
Traveling nowhere far,
When a girl looked in, saw him, and screamed.
It was funny yet embarrassing.

Plague mask guy rarely says a word,
And those he says cannot be heard.
He snaps pictures with people for their Tumblr;
He'll one day be the latest Tik Tok wonder.

He goes around causing such a scene
As people stare or laugh obscene.
The mess he makes is so much fun.
Yes, plague mask guy is for everyone.

Galaxy Boy

There's a galaxy boy I know
Who I tend to worry about.
He spent his time chasing a goddess
Who treated him like a lout.
He then befriended her anyways,
Hoping to change her mind.
She took his hand
And made him fall in line.
Galaxy Boy holds the secret to the world,
Both yours and mine,
But he's stuck with the goddess,
So no secrets he finds.
The goddess says she loves him now.
I believe that's a lie.
She'll drop him. He'll fall to earth
And begin to cry.
I hope when he finds that time,
When he starts to fall,
He'll remember my little poem
And know he's worth it all.
A false god is fun for short,
But when she goes away,
Galaxy Boy will be himself,
And hopefully, he'll stay.

Summer's Tip

Summer expectations, ones we can't seem to shake.
Skyscraper standards we could never recreate.
We left the kitchen table, abandoned school,
In hopes of racing to the pool.

Back when bug bites were our concern
And offered lessons were better unlearned.
When the casualties of wasting a day
Was in favor of the memories we now replay.

That's what I want to relive,
Where I want to be: summer's tip.
But now the prospect of being carefree
Leaves me with an itchy anxiety.
The blended days, washed away,
Now leave a stinging pain.

So despite my need to relive simplicity,
I'm stuck working in a busy city.
Surrounded by fleeting moments
And dreams ready to be broken,
I no longer await summer's tip.
Instead, I see it as a looming cliff,
Past which is uncertainty and dread.
My golden summers left for dead.

A Joker in a Saint's Skin

You seemed like a fun time yet so down to earth.
You looked so joyful and so unnerved.
But what happens when the curtain falls?
If behind the mask you're not real at all?
You kept a steady pace until no example was set.
You had a heavy hand till there's no mark on your head.
What if I've wasted time on all your facade,
and I still want you more. Come on, what are the odds?
If all my heart's wants were for a terrible friend,
my disappointment is when I know you're a joker in a
saint's skin.
While I was dreaming of being perfect (like you),
I was missing how your jokes were cruel.
You set an example and abandoned it there
The second the social pressure teared.
What if I threw out my own achievements for yours
While you were wrapping the church's doors?
You were a pedestal that no one could reach;
Now you're a caution parents will teach.
And yet I waste my time on your facades,
And I want you more against all the odds!
If all my deep dreams were for a terrible friend,
Why am I disappointed by a joker in a saint's skin?
And now I'm tearing hair out, wishing you could see
Your childlike behaviors and tendencies.

Time to Stop

We were by the fountain wishing we could jump in,
But it was too cold.
Taking pictures, we looked like a dream.
Fill up the night, pouring out screams,
Before it got old.

Oh, and up at night wondering what life will be like at
eighteen.
Quoting a movie, Legally Blonde, answering questions
we can't get wrong.
Just let me be in my memory.

Take me back, back to Savannah,
Dressing up, forgetting our manners.
On River Street wasting our day,
Giving all our time away.
Take me back to when I was carefree
Before I paid my royalties.
When the beach was a nearby stop,
I wanted time to stop.

Made a vacay a musical, ate up our company, got full.
But that's done.
I can feel my sunburn, another page I can't unturn.
Was it worth the fun?

Maybe Best Friend

Less than ten minutes away is my maybe best friend.
Less than ten minutes away is someone on which I could
depend.

They don't know how much I have to offer or how much
I want to give.
They live a few blocks over, just beyond the ridge.

They could come over anytime if they just let me know;
For them, I would be willing to brave the snow.

Less than ten minutes away is someone I would confide
my fears in.
My maybe best friend would only have to listen.

Then I would listen, too, and they would find
Just how much wonder there is inside my mind.

So Maybe Best Friend, if you got my letter,
Reach out, let me know, and we can get better.

Senior Year

Summer nears, a chapter ends.
Final moments scattered in the winds.

A pair of nice heels, a car of songs,
And the feeling that nothing could go wrong.
Despite the cults, cliques, and naysayers,
It was a game of mostly fun players.
Hair flying, hands joined, feet in the air.
Despite the party poopers, we had no care.

Then hats flew, like a vision of three weeks.
But unlike then, no tears drop or sad word speaks.
We laugh off another cult. We're not yet grown
and go our own way, still not alone.
Time nears and will not stop;
We cannot outrun the clock.
So we sit and wait inside a car,
Enjoying the minutes that now seem so far.

Yet once competitions are over and the curtain's down,
Will I begin to fear the once happy town?
Now full of fading memories and once-happy thoughts
Is a brain of sorrow that now rots.

It's not over yet, though it still nears.
But isn't the future filled with excitement over fears?

The Age of Friendships

I had a best friend in kindergarten.
There were large gaps when I didn't see him.
My other best friend had her own crowd.
Who didn't like me and said so out loud.

My mother's friend had a girl my brother's age,
And the one constant was the war we waged.
Our joint friend was a manipulator,
And we found our friendship when we lost her.

One day I ran to her in the church parking lot
To tell her the news that made my happiness rot.
"I'm moving away," I said with a cry.
"I have to leave and say my goodbyes."
We spent our last moments giggling about a crush.
Our last true connection was a happiness rush.

My first new friend was made to fit;
My mom introduced us and told us to sit.
But she had a million friends and I had her.
It wasn't until recently our bond felt sure.

I had a maybe friend who's now a dear one,
But her then-best friend hated my fun.
She slammed doors in my face and despised my revenge.
While she was in the group, our friendship was tinged.

Then I started a new school and got a new group.
I was amidst, yet apart, from the rest of the coop.

There some friendships started but few last.
Now all of those memories are in the past.

In the midst of my struggles, I had a penpal:
A colorful soul, an interesting gal.
Hiding behind a pen, I could reveal
All of the things I happened to feel.

By the end of middle school, I was friends with a mirror
Whose reflection was mine, though my emotions were
clearer.
I half knew her friends and wanted to know more,
But all of this took place before.

My friend stood by while I was a curse.
She's still there through better and worse.
She tells me her loves, her works, and her drama.
I tell her how much I wish to beat karma.

I once had a friend for whom I vastly cared—
A mirror whose secrets she never shared.
But it's hard to love glass, for it never gives.
So I left; in pain is now how I live.

In my hurt, I found more who love, just as I.
They're open and honest about how much they cry.
In my new flock, we're not much alike.
We have more understanding than we have spite.

During coffee shop meetings and idle park talks,
I gained a friend who can outrun my walks.

She's strong and firm in what she believes,
And she keeps a joy for all who see.

My pen pal now sees me face to face.
For each other, we'd run to any place.
Now her friends are mine, too, and here to stay.
I'm the first clapping at the end of each play.

Now my best friend lives only a few miles
And is willing to not talk for a while.
My other friend is here to hype me up.
Her overflow fills my cup.

I have friends whom I've never seen
And others who go for drives with me.
I have some who check up despite a lack of trust.
I have friends who calm me down when they must.

So through highs and lows and all I've lost,
I think I'm okay with how much it cost.
There are people in my life I love more than they know,
But after our time on stage, I hope it shows.
Despite the hate that bubbles underneath,
I still have too much love to sheath.

7. For No One But Myself

A thought from 2018

The longing to see more light.
The calm knowing of near ending strife.
The knowledge of brightness on the other side.
The spark of light in someone's eyes.
It draws you in and holds you near.
It makes the darkness run in fear.
This one thing decides all fate;
It makes the spark come to take.
No other thing can hold a match
To the spark of hope so prone to latch.

Take Me to the Gardens

Take me to the gardens to admire all the beauty,
And maybe when I look up, you'll be looking at me.
Take me on a walk, and I'll think of the faes I wrote of,
The ones I get lost looking for, the ones that I love.
Lose me among the tulips as I lie down for a nap,
And find me in the daisies or covered in tree sap.
Follow me through the gazebos, the middle of the square,
And watch as a stray flower ends up stuck in my hair.
Kiss me by the camellias, bloom like my emotions,
Then point down the rabbit trail we hope to get lost in.
Take me to see the sunflowers, somehow taller than I,
And tell me what you believe they'd see if they had eyes.
Maybe I'll get lost in the gardens, looking through the
weeds,
And maybe, if you're watching, I'll steal a couple seeds.
Think of me like the babbling stream that flows through
the plants
And then decide to take of me and hold my hand.
You'll soon lose me in a drawing that I drew for myself.
Remind me to breathe in fresh air, better for my health.
Paint me like a flower and try and keep me here alive
Because we are still young and hoping that we'll survive.

Take me to the gardens where my hope is alive,
'Cause there amongst the wildest things, I begin to thrive.

Escape From Reality

My brain is like a garden full of helpful seeds,
But now I'm recognizing that most of them are weeds.
I have so much to plant now, but so much cluttering.
The garden that reads "for rent" is less inspiring.
I started this piece hours ago in the Sacramento shops,
But now I'm hiding in Florida; I'm at a different stop.
From California poppies to orange-blossomed trees,
I like to go wherever the media takes me.
From poison oak gardens with a skinny black cat
To somewhere in Manhattan in an amateur chef's flat,
My adventures can take me many places
That later live in my mind's spaces.
Like right now, it's a dreary gray, hanging cumulus cloud
day,
And I hang in the garden where faes may stay.
But next week, I'm high amongst the stars
Or driving a Boston bridge in my uncle's car.
Tomorrow I'll be in the gazebo of a colonial garden.
The day after that, I'm scowling at my warden.
Weather changes, and so do I;
People revive with a little rewind.
Because my memories are set in pages,
I can look back on all the ages.
I pick up a book, and I'm whisked away
To all the places I wish I could stay.
Maybe one day I'll have finished this piece,
But for now, we'll have to wait and …

In The Meadow

I'm here among the wildflowers:
Now I'm truly alive.
I'm here among the dry brush:
Like them, I thrive.
Burn me and I rot away
Like any thriving thing
But leave me be and let me go,
And I begin to sing.

A Poem For Me

For myself, I have little words.
The ones I had were iced and now hurt.
At one point, my words made life ideal.
Words like "special" and "priceless" now sound unreal.
Once I grew, the words turned sharp:
"Unwanted," "unloved," and others began to harp.
I numbered them out. Now all words are gone—
A sanctuary and a choir now without a song.
Some words come from other places:
"Hey, I love you," friendly faces.
But I've heard those empty words from people I loved,
Words like that my numbness wants to shove.

I like myself, so don't cry for me,
For I am not miserable.
But all the words inside my head
Are twisted and jumbled.

Past Self

When you're six feet under, I won't cry.
I won't stop by to say goodbye.
You know that I cannot go back,
'Cause you were the eleventh hour, my fade to black.

"I'm Fine"

"How are you feeling?" Well, I'm feeling really terrible.
I hate the feeling that I'm always on the centerfold.
I hate the facade I feel like I have to show.
I hate the reason that I hate being called beautiful.

"How are you doing?" Well, I'm doing as well as I can,
But being honest, I don't really have a plan.
I hate regretting that I even have a man.
I hate the fact I can't stand holding his hand.

"What's going on with you?" Do you even care?
Do you even take notice that I'm not there?
Do you feel my presence around you, everywhere?
Do you even care that my life isn't fair?

"I'll see you later." No, you never will.
'Cause even as we're speaking, I'm on the windowsill.
I shake the thoughts away and swallow down my pill.
I breathe in relief as the thoughts go still.

"Talk to you later!" Please keep checking in.
You have no idea the way my head begins to spin.
I can feel like an outsider in my own skin,
But this is a battle I'll fight to win.

Muse

I'd like to say my muse is Mother Nature,
That her breath inspires the words I write.
But my real muse is my own pain.
I am moved by my own spite.

Whereas I once wrote of happy things,
The hope I felt in the midst of spring,
Now I write of my own spirit of dread
And how the one who pained me left me for dead.
They didn't notice I was gone,
And they still can't see what they did wrong.
My pain is killing me, soft but sure.
I want them to kill me quick, no more time in this world.

I have more pain with newer friends,
And feelings blossomed that I thought would end.
He looked me in the eye and kept a steady smile.
All those feelings rushed back from once in a while.
But he's not mine; he belongs to another.
So all of this love I try to smother.

So yes, my love, Nature's no longer a muse.
For pain works better as a lit fuse.

Why Can't I?

Why can't I
Find the emotion I'm holding close to my breast?
Why can't I
Cry to the song? Is it wrong to hope for the best?

I broke down today, trying to find my way.
I lost myself caring for something more than my health.
I lost a friend. I always knew that it would happen. Again.

I didn't like feeling stupid again.
I was hoping I would gain a friend.
I keep thinking that it's plain to see.
But this isn't about me.

Why can't I
Find the emotion I'm holding close to my breast?
Why can't I
Cry to the song? Is it wrong to hope for the best?

Maybe

Maybe I'll amount to nothing.

Maybe one day, I'll just die.

Maybe I'm just a waste of ink and graphite.

Maybe all I ever do is lie.

Maybe I've ruined every relationship.

Maybe the voice is right: I'm truly alone.

Maybe I'll get a thousand cats.

Maybe I'm waiting by the phone.

Maybe you hate me like "I hate you."

Maybe this burning feeling gets stronger.

Maybe the rumors you started are true.

Maybe my past lasts longer.

Maybe tomorrow I stay in my bed.

Maybe I never wake to begin.

Maybe my sleep will last a thousand years.

Maybe I'm gone and won't be missed.

Maybe my curse will last forever.

Maybe I'm not trying to get better.

Maybe I did this to myself.

Maybe you'll send me a letter.

Maybe one day I'll be happy.

Maybe one day I'll be okay.

Maybe I'll make it: I'll be alive.

Maybe someday I'll come out to play.

Tears

Release. I've been let go after so much holding back.

Peace. I'm falling down, leaving sad, salty tracks.

Alone. I fall to the ground from higher peaks.

Known. That I'm wanted even though you leave streaks.

Fears. They can hide and be repressed.

Tears. Some unwanted, but needed nonetheless.

Crashing Down

I feel like I don't want to know what I'll be.

I feel like I should always be smiling.

I feel like I should be the best at my job.

And then a former friend comes along.

She did good, and I guess that's great.

Now it's myself that I hate.

I wanna be heard when I sing,

But maybe I should find a new thing.

When there's no praise, I feel no worth.

But when I'm praised, it's empty words.

Maybe I'm too hard on myself.

And now I have bad mental health.

Maybe I'll never be enough.

I just wish it was myself I loved.

8. Inspired

You

You make me feel lost like a minute in time.

Yet not out of place: a dolphin in the Rhine.

You make me feel uncomfortable with your jests.

I feel out of place looking nice in jean vests.

I dread seeing you, yet I await your call.

I feel out of time like I'm an old mall.

I'm lost, with or without you at my side,

Yet when you're near me, I go and hide.

Abandon me to die, and maybe I can thrive.

Even if you leave me, I'm still alive.

How can I tell you the secrets that I hide?

How can I author what will be your demise?

Always and forever can somehow fall apart.

I'm left all alone like an old shopping cart.

Heritage

My history is in hayfields,

My heritage is acres.

I hold what my past yields.

All of these old waymakers.

My family owned land here,

Yet I feel no connection.

Those who gather here?

Those are my congregation.

Unfathomable

You cannot fathom what I can do.

Trust me, my dear, you have no clue.

I am a caterpillar meant for the sky;

I'm a clown who's born to cry.

You cannot put a giraffe in a tree;

You shall not try to classify me.

I'm a ship that's meant to ride on the wind;

I'm the trickster you've dubbed "a godsend."

I can be fear, and I can be love.

I can bring peace like a dove.

But oh, my dear, don't try to imagine

The things you cannot fathom.

For I leave disaster in my wake:

I can give, and I shall take.

Let me in, and good things grow,

Or watch me burn and start to know:

My little jokes were so much more.

I am the rain about to pour.

I am a tragic comedy,

So please do not imagine me.

Homes

Our house on eagle way had marigolds.

My mother pruned them when things got cold.

We found a kitten in our flower bed,

Then let her in to rest her head.

They both followed us to two towers,

That little cat and those orange flowers.

My brother and I ate weeds in the backyard.

We caught butterflies or swam, and life wasn't hard.

Sometimes stickers got stuck on our feet.

Then mom consoled us with something sweet.

Our toys would fly over our fence

And fell off the cliff, lost in the mist.

Summer's one oh one was too dry for mud,

But fall came, and the parking lots flood.

Back at home, there was a tree.

At the top were some scraggly leaves.

I always watched it from my window

And always prayed that it would grow.

When we last went back to see,

My heart filled with so much glee.

The tree's full girthy body stood on its own,

The full outcome of a good childhood home.

Anxieties

A trillion thorns prick my chest.

Blood oozes from my breast.

Maybe I'll bleed out and be a river.

Rivers are loved, for they can deliver.

My heart is about to burst.

Soon the rest of me will disperse.

Maybe my body will become the graceful wind.

People love a breeze; the stream is a godsend.

Maybe I'll melt into unknown,

Lost forever to be a shadow.

People rely on shadow more than they think.

They need somewhere to hide, somewhere to slink.

These feelings, too, shall pass,

But right now, it seems to last.

So let me bleed, or burst, or melt for now,

Then bring me back and tell me how

I am loved, relied on, and cherished.

Today is not the day I shall perish.

Peace and War

Behind my eyes is a lavender field

Where all my worldly troubles yield.

Sometimes it's blue. Sometimes it's gray.

It sometimes lets me stay all day.

But sometimes, the sky is overcast,

And I get caught up in the past.

When lightning strikes and splits the sky,

The sky herself begins to cry.

Then the stalks droop and petals fall,

And the field is lost behind a wall.

I'm on the other side, lost in a chasm.

And a lavender field I can no longer fathom.

But when the rain ends and the sky returns

And my lesson has been learned,

I'll see past the wall, and it will yield

Till I'm once again in a lavender field.

The Road of Life

All that has accumulated to be me is still there.

No matter how I try to trim the train, it won't tear.

All of my experiences follow in my wake,

Even the ones I didn't want to take.

The road I walked on, the one that got me here,

Is broken, full of potholes, but smoother as it nears.

No journey has been easy, everyone knows

The grief that can trail behind always shows.

So if my past drags on behind me, at least the future's

bright.

Past mistakes may shine through, but I've forgone spite.

For once, this path is no longer mine.

I want the newcomer to enjoy their time.

The elders plowed the field to give me space,

And now on my road, others can race.

Each generation makes a change,

So the next one has a wider range.

If all of me has led to this road,

I hope someone else takes it to the unknown.

They'll have trial and strife,

But hopefully an easier life.

Accidents

Shall accidents make us men?
Or do they render us human?

If a slip-up is a sin,

Then I, too, have fallen.

What's done is done, despite the cause.

You can't take back what is lost.

Yet not all mistakes are a downfall;

Some choose not to answer the call.

If what's spilled could be a masterpiece,

Then I see no wrong in loving the least.

If it was all for naught, then so was I.

I'll leave you behind as you cry.

Yet accidents can be a happy thing.

An unwanted child begins to sing.

If they found a voice in the middle of despair,

Maybe my voice can be repaired.

An accident may have broken my stride,

But another gave me my pride.

Maybe I was a product of yesterday,

But that day has ended; the sun now plays.

Among the disasters and fixtures of the land,

Fate lends a willing hand.

9. Fall

A Rainy Week

It's been raining for a week,

A streamy, stringing, freezing feat.

I wanted the sun to warm my skin,

But it's dull and cold, and there's wind.

You say your mom won't let you play.

It's muddy, not sunny: it's a fuddy day.

I saw my friend at the park with her.

They're laughing, running, and feeling sure.

I'm stuck at school not doing work.

Feeling alone, missing home, I feel so hurt.

Maybe our sunny days were truly a drizzle.

Then they popped, our fun stopped, a flopped sizzle.

Maybe next week the star comes out to see me,

But the wet makes me feel decked. My respect is dreary.

A Ghost's Lullaby

When you pass by the cemetery,

I hope you're thinking of me.

'Cause a part of me died long ago,

And now I'm just a lonely ghost.

Among the autumn leaves and the frigid air,

A part of me loves it here.

With the dying grass and the summertime,

Is the sound of a mournful cry:

A ghost's lullaby

When you pass by the graveyard,

Remember that life's hard.

But death is forever,

And I miss rolling in clover

And running in the rain and getting to eat,

Falling in love and getting cold feet,

And all the things that pass you by

As a passerby.

And I'm gone, so far gone from emotions

But I keep watching and hoping

For the way, the way tomorrow could bring,

A life to someone or something.

Born to Die

Picture me macabre
From the dust and to the dark.
Fathom me remarkable
In my grave near the park.

All my life, I've been followed
By the one who holds the scythe.
Their lullaby haunts my wake.
I'll always remember what they say:

"You think you have it rough
Here in your little despairing pit,
But, my dear, you have it easy,
And you don't know the half of it."

"You won't die from a battle,
Neither on the front or real," he croons,
"You'll die being piteous,
A bud that will never bloom."

So now I lie, waiting
In my grave on my hill.
As dusk still falls, so will I.
Await my fate, born to die.

10. To the disappointing

A Journey Through a Maze

This poem uses flower language 2

I wake up in a dream wandering through a flower maze
With four of my old friends, each a recognizable face.
As we walk through ivy, dotted with lilacs and yellow
tulips,
I can't help but look back at the entrance, feeling foolish.
Magdalina, you waltzed among the candytuft towers.
Joy, you amongst the amaryllis flowers,
While Katarina smelled the coreopsis blossoms
And Amelie picked aster with great caution.
I myself was caught up in the poppy,
And when I looked up, you were walking without me.
We wander through the foraged halls,
Our voices bouncing off leafy walls.
But one voice falls silent all too quick.
My voice is gone. You never noticed it.
We came to a four-way with different directions,
And had to decide which to get lost in.
Katerina suggested the path of columbine petals
As Magdalina chose the abatina and nettles.
I suggested the road of sweet basil,
But Joy chose the borage for our travel.
You four began to point out the arborvitae trees.
I couldn't help but notice the dead zinnia leaves.
We then break into an open, airy meadow
With a plethora of blossoms in the morning glow.
Magdalina picks some wild rose.
Joy chooses calla lily before the blossoms close.

Katerina and Amelie both make bouquets
Of apple blossoms and geraniums the color of blue jays.
They gift them to each other as they claim they're best
friends.
The rest of us just watch, wondering when this will end.
Magdalina picks purple and yellow hyacinth as I notice the
begonias.
Amelie finds the daisy and yellow jasmine and gets lost in
the aroma.
When it's time to leave and once again feel lost,
They go one way, but I wonder about the cost.
I hand Joy one last sprig of tansy and butterfly weed,
But she doesn't care about the seed.
In my heart, rosemary blooms,
But valerian leaves its perfumes.
I wander alone yet don't feel lost.
I am no longer wondering the cost.
I have new friends like the white rose,
Who's there for any problem life may pose.
There are daisies who bring me joy along my path
And happy marigolds who will always have my back.
The sunflowers are there whenever I need a friend,
And the lotus and African violets can be such a godsend.
I don't walk alone: now bluebonnets dot my way.
I guess I'm glad I went my separate way.

Teachers and Weeds

You, Bindweed, mislabeled me.
You put me in a box and told me to sing.
You, Dandelion, you worked me too hard.
You dress yourself up just to fall apart.
Bindweed and Dandelion, you monsters in charge,
You told us we were animals, while you were at large.

You, Wild Carrot, were a strange case.
You came and left with no remains.
Your offspring, too, were wild weeds
With poison words as their seeds.
Your eccentricness seemed like fun,
Until you got mad that no work was done.

Then the Burdock thought he was so smart,
But I learned little on his part.
Don't get me wrong, it's not his fault,
But his class wasn't worth its salt.

So far, Golden Rod hasn't taught me much,
Just things I'd forgotten and others such.
But Golden Rod has a pretty name,
So maybe the future isn't so plain.

Then there was You, Kudzu, most cruel.
You came into my mind and overgrew.
You acted like it was Rose's fault, then mine,
When leaving you in charge was the true crime.
You acted like we just needed tightened stitches,

But I guess you changed your mind when you called us
[   ].

Greek Goddess

I'm not doing you any favors.
Your complexion of a savior
Is too much to drag me down.
I won't say you're trying too hard
Or try and get you a get-well card.
I liked you better before you looked like a clown.

Who are you trying to impress?
You go around looking so stressed.
You should relax; we already know you're modest.
You work so darn much
But he's already in your clutch.
You'll be just another goddess, burnt up at your hottest.
Greek goddess.

The world still bows to you.
I don't need your stinking clue
To know you're just unbothered.
You're just a teacher's pet,
Leave and then get left,
Downing in your own water.

I hope you know you were too fake.
You spent too long in silence to get me awake.
You'll lose your friend right as the world ends,
The tale you spin to help you win.

Role Model

I remember when you used to be my role model,
When the respect I had made my common sense topple.
And I remember how it felt when you disappeared.
I remember when I always sought you first,
Asking silent questions for answers I never heard,
And I forget what it was like with you here.

Now you're just the mother of a friend.
Not a saint, or a savior, or a godsend.
You didn't keep it up, ask or care,
And I don't see you anywhere.

What happened to the overflowing well I knew of?
The one so eager to fill my cup.
Did you run dry or just stop?
I know dependence isn't something I need to be okay,
But I could use a prop-up just for today.
I guess I'll never get to the top.

Now you're forever away and long gone.
I guess you'll never be honored with this song.
I hope you know I remember your name,
But now my life is more of the same.

To make an impact, you have to pursue.
Don't give up on me; I need help too.
There's revival; I wanna be renewed.
But it's too late to get that from you.

Over it

What is trust if it is broken
When you no longer have someone to hope in?
I hope you know I hoped for change.
That was before I knew you were deranged.
It's not fair to call you insane,
But I was dying, and you promised rain.
Goodbye, I guess. Have fun with *her*.
You're just another person I didn't mean to hurt.
Do not fret, I'll leave you be,
But you are not a part of me.

What is a lie without the truth
When the incoherent is left loose?
If your beloved missed the side I had to tell,
Then why would I think you'd share as well?
So I hope your romance grows on false love.
If you're waiting for a sign, I send no dove.
I hope you both hurt as I once did.
You'll get no more words. I'm over it.

Fleeing Thought

I guess it hasn't hit that you're not here anymore.
Like any minute now, you're walking through that door.
I guess I'm still waiting on some promises,
But now they appear to just be wishes.

11. Those I loved

First Loves

Oh, First Loves, oh apple blossom blooms,
You came my way, then disappeared,
Gone all too soon.

Oh, First Crush, a tedious affair.
Too many days, too many weeks,
Were wasted on my prayers.
I hoped that you would see me,
But now that hope is gone.
You, First Crush, were a poppy,
Somewhere in my mind, lost in the throng.

Oh, Old Friend, you're a daisy true.
You make me smile, make me laugh,
But that love is not for you.
You and the Wild Rural Flowers
Made such a lovely pair.
I was not jealous. I did not cower.
I was a joyful spare.

Oh you, The Deserter, a true wild card.
Not meant for her, nor me,
Yet we fell hard.
You are like Venus' trap,
A miserable surprise.
You're sweet words like comb's sap;
You made a throne of lies.
I graciously told my heart to stop;
I would not dare succumb.

But then she fell, and two on top,
And you left them numb.

Then you, oh Daffodil, you were never here.
We liked each other but then did not.
You appear and disappear.

You, Blue Bonnet, stayed for years.
In my mind, no passerby,
Yet I began to fear.
Though I admired all your flaws,
You left me to stare.
Now you're in another's claws,
And I know you don't care.
Yet I wonder if amidst your petals
A hidden stem we might share.
That could break down these walls.

Then you, oh Pine, so evergreen,
You were always there.
Yet your nettles leaves aren't what they seem.
Your laughs were just that,
So you left me behind.
And when you came back,
You didn't drop a line.

Then you, Dear Stranger, you're kudzu:
You came, and you conquered,
You then overgrew.
I didn't like you, but I suspected.
Then you confessed and caused me stress.

I felt confused, I felt conflicted,
But I gave you hard news nonetheless.

Then you, oh Laughing Rose, were here.
Through our peaked anxieties and scars,
We kept together, near.
Maybe you'll wilt, maybe I'll leave,
Or we fall apart too soon.
But we're wide awake, and I can see
We've just begun to bloom.

3 Weeks

You came and picked up my brother today,
And as the two of you were on your way,
I thought about those twenty-one days.

Do you remember making me weak?
Up all night texting, I got no sleep.
But even though it had to go, I always think:
"I wonder if he remembers those three weeks?"

Broken Toys

Our church had a broken toy car track,
But the toy car's wheels seemed to lack.
Its tiny toy driver would steer off course;
He did it on purpose and made himself worse.
I wanted to help but never did.
He's poisoned now, little toy kid.

I once made friends with a little wooden horse,
Who then, one day, ran off the course.
Once off the course, he didn't go back.
He wanted to stray from the track.
I'm the one who kept him alive.
But, at the moment, he doesn't thrive.

I know a toy, a stuffed sloth,
Who seems warm and fuzzy, made of cloth.
But inside him, the stuffing's bad.
He won't throw it out; it's all he had.
Yet I don't abandon him;
I'm not sure it's just a whim.

There's a stuffed frog who tries to ploy,
But his own life he destroys.
I think I'm done with broken boys.

Crushes

Do you like me?
Can you tell me? 'Cause I need to know.
Do you think I'm cute or just so-so?

Do you think of me at night and get butterflies?
Do you like me?
Tell me, 'cause I think you might.

Can we get it out in the open?
Can we make it plain as day?
Can you tell me? 'Cause I'm hoping
To know what you'll say.

'Cause you're in my mind
From time to time, not just a passerby.
And oh, you're like me—
A shoulder I could use to cry.

Should I text you first?
Will you text me back?
Will you make me have a heart attack?

Will you help me up
When I'm feeling down?
In a year from now,
Will you be around?

For the Siren

I don't know if this is fleeting.
Either way, I'd like to explore.
But you, I could not ruin;
You could outlast my storm.

Talk to me with nice words,
Even as you let me down,
So I'm not disappointed,
Just sad you're not around.

Call me, let me hear your voice,
When you go away.
I'll stop my anxieties,
So you'll maybe want to stay.

Come home when you get the chance.
We'd love to see your face.
Don't leave me lonely; I need a friend.
Please leave me with a trace.

12. Winter

The Eve Before

One dying leaf clings to the tree,
One last hope I offer to thee.
For though your tree is mostly barren,
Your chest can still expand.
Though mist tries to obscure the view,
There is still a song for you.
Through your sweat, tears, and many yawns,
You persevered until the dawn.
So cling once more to the unknown.
It's not yet done; we're not yet home.
Continue to stay. Please don't let go.
With the new year comes new hope.

New Year's Day

With a new season, new changes come too.
New moss grows—old made new.
Even what's dead can bring new life.
Rain brings new growth. Growth comes from strife.
New year, new me.
New heartbreak and tragedy.
New life, new hope.
We'll no longer need to cope.
If moss can grow, then so can I.
Look back for once and no longer cry.

13. We Fell Apart

Peace

Maybe because you brought no peace,
Leaving *us* set me at ease.

Lost/Known

What is it to be lost in the midst of being known?
It's like ignoring a call and crying at the dial tone.
I'm here all alone.

I wander through an empty town, alive with memories.
People pass by me like ghosts. They keep ignoring me
As if I'm a dream.

Maybe I am a ghost. Maybe I am truly dead.
Maybe all those poisonous thoughts really got into my
head.
It's because of what you said.

You told me that you cared; That was the first warning
sign
Because you only cared until I started to cry.
You were my demise.

I know now I don't need people, so I watch them leave.
I watch as your clique falls apart, the outcome I had
foreseen.
I'm sorry, that's mean.

I am not alone, though it can often feel that way.
Friends can come and go. They might leave me by the
end of today.
Regardless, I say:
Let me lean on you as you lean on me in tandem.

I'll love things you don't love about yourself, things I
can't fathom
I'll write your anthem.

I'll lie in the road and accept my demise with grace.
I'm already in my funeral clothes, decked out in old lace.
Please don't give me space.

Smother me in tender love but try to let me breathe.
Give me warning for the fateful day when you will have
to leave;
Last trick up your sleeve.

Maybe I'll make it out alive, going through phases
Of different people and lifestyles; different faces.
They still leave traces
Of who I was before I found out I'm meant to be:
Someone who can let go and who knows what it costs to
be free.
Yet I am still me.

I once cursed you for pulling me off my path, I was
wrong.
Turns out I needed to walk that way, even though it's
long.
New morning, new song.

Last night I felt lost amongst acquaintances I have.
Yet as I danced joyfully, I began to laugh.
I'm on a new path.

You were alone of sorts, while I had many friends near,
Yet I did not hate or pity you. I let the air then clear.
You are still my peer.

I drew you in to dance with me and had a good time.
But for the rest of my tale to be told, you don't fit the
rhyme.
I'll see you in line.

I'm not sorry that we have begun to drift away.
That day when I drove away, I made our drift a
conscious break.
I'll no longer fake.

Now I drift by the gravestones of friends I used to have.
I'll gaze on yours and reminisce of the days you made me
sad.
I will no longer be mad.
I am glad of all I have and have had.

Downfall

I have so much I owe to you; greeting cards with empty
words.
We went to coffee shops for the view and forced smiles
in cast pictures.
You don't belong here! Why are you here?
You make up rules and expect us to adhere.
I'll be honest—you pissed me off more than I can say.
You say that this is love. It's a game you play.
Do you realize we're no longer friends?
Do you know I orchestrated the end?
You have your group of friends, one you can "trust,"
I'm staring at the church steeple, knowing they're full of
lust.
I don't know why I'm enraged,
But your lack of emotions is staged.
Mannequins like you don't make much of what I want
'Cause plastic isn't human touch. I don't need your
stunts.
Your entourage will fall apart,
I've seen the teases.
I myself have fallen apart.
I'm picking up my pieces.

But you were horses and men to me,
So when you break, I'll have no sympathy.

Poem #12

I thought you were better than this.
I knew my pettiness was too extreme.
You handled me with flawlessness.
But let's be honest, that was mean.

A look from the arctic numbed me.
I had thought you summer, no ice queen.
But now I wonder if you ever cared;
If your empty words could have been spared.

Do you even know how much I cherished you?
Did my eleven poems give you no clue?
It doesn't matter, this should be the last.
I'm sorry, old friend; you'll be in the past.

This Wave Will Crash

I can't get you out of my head.
You've taken root and begun to spread.
I'm counting down days until you're uprooted.
You know I can't stand you. It's so stupid.
The fact my apathy consumes my time,
While you get by feeling fine.

Even if I feel you don't deserve him,
I don't want him for me.
I want you to feel the way I felt:
Angry and full of apathy.

So for you at this moment, there's no well wishes.
You're a sink I'll abandon full of dirty dishes.
Have fun with the filth, it's not mine to deal with
anymore.
I hope I spread in your mind. This wave will crash on
your shore.

Former Friend

I hope my pen's like a bullet in your heart
That makes you shatter, fall completely apart.
I hope my words do what your silence did to me:
I hope it leaves you dying in a pit full of apathy.

I hope that you'll disappear,
And when you think of me, you'll think of here.
I hope that you get left behind too.
But unlike me, they won't find you.
In your heart, there should be a hole
Where you left me an unfulfilled role.

I hope you know you sucked as a friend.
I hope this suffering in me will end.
I don't want to see you anymore,
So I'm leaving out the door.
Maybe I'm obsessed with you,
But that girl is dead. That time is through.

You're in the past. I'm moving on.
But you should know that you were wrong.
Your silence drove me away.
You had your games you tried to play.
So when I left, it was for good.
You can't fix us. You never could.

Pleasure

Why does one spread themselves thin
Fighting a battle they can never win?
Why does one try and overexert?
It's themselves they always hurt.
No matter how you try, you can't cool a wasteland.
The effort itself hurts none but your own hand.
So why bother and please every soul
When it's your own that grows a hole?
Why try and be the hero when villains hate you
nonetheless?
Why try and make her see when it just causes you
stress?
So take a step and a breathe and try to move on,
You'll soon forget the way you were wronged.
If focusing on fixing it destroys yourself,
Leave it behind and focus on your health.
If they start to flounder, then they'll see
How much they had once needed thee.

Our Old News

A year ago, I would have given you a limb.
Two, I considered you a best friend.
All the notes and cards now fall void.
All those messages are useless noise.
You once cared about my self-isolation,
And your life was a place I wanted to be in.
That's why it hurt: because I cared.
And when I left, you only stared.
I made a choice. You made yours.
Now that past is behind locked doors.

14. The Passerby

A Bouquet of Roses and Baby's Breath

Miss Swift used roses to show the love she had,
But for me, they symbolize something bad.
They sat in my cup holder as I drove home.
A part of me wished they would fly out the window.
Flowers are like relationships: they come with seasons.
Both can bloom, thrive, and then die,
And when they inevitably do, someone cries.
So showing up with a bouquet seemed like an omen,
Like a grim appearing when I've begun hoping.
After a night of awkward laughter swimming in my
head,
I was left resenting flowers, wishing they were dead.
I last received a rose at my angel's relative's funeral,
Back then, I'd opened it for faes, pretending they were
real.
But these sit on a shelf in my room
Causing joy, confusion, and gloom.
I refuse to look at their rosy faces.
In fact, at the moment, I'm turned away.
Do you know that this relationship is intended for
death?
Or were you just focused on a bouquet of roses and
baby's breath?
I'm not saying it will end soon.
I'm not saying I'll give in to the gloom,
But I'm a realist, and when I look at bouquets,
I see rushed commitment followed by dark days.

All Good Things …

They lie dead upon my bathroom floor.
Cold and limp for forever and more.
The last remnants from an okay night,
Other than a few foggy memories and frostbite.
Now gone, ready to be incinerated,
Just the way I'd anticipated.
Maybe I was wrong to commit this murder.
But maybe that okay night was a precursor
To the inevitable act I would commit
And where the body now sits.

Scarlet red covers the tile—
A color I've hated for a while.
A thin body and scarce limbs,
The last remains of my committed sins.
My commitment resentment was the true death
Of what was once a happy place in my head.
My love, once alive, suddenly froze
And now lays dead alongside the rose.

Our End

Is my death worth there only being us?
Is it worth the wishful lust?
My demise was a price for too high.
But you were willing to live a lie.
If I'm dead, how are you okay?
Have you even noticed I've passed away?
Even now, my body and attitude grow cold,
Yet it's my hand you long to hold.
My hints tell you I'm the monster, yet you don't see.
In the end, only I will be relieved.

Song: Villain

How do I tell you I'm happy,
But I don't see this lasting?
How do I tell you I'm drowning?
I guess I won't. I'm cowardly.

What if I'm the villain, villain.
My deeds are on the page last written.
You choose a time, I'll choose the settin',
And in the end, I'll lose a friend.
'Cause I'm the villain, villain. Yeah.

How do I tell you I've got a bad backstory?
Do you not notice my allegory?
I'd throw you out the window, mirror my son's fate.
I'll blow out candles when it's not my cake.
It's not my choice, though I first spoke:
This too will end, the way I wrote.

You dug your own grave, but I took the shot.
You'll have no pain, I've had a lot.
And in the end, the villain dies.
And the hero's story gets revised.

My own goals now seem twisted.
I see myself as wicked.
My choice was a one-way ticket.

Changes

Take me to the place where good things grow.
Show me hope, peace, and love,
The joys I'd never know.

Show me the world through your lashes, like I did mine.
I showed you all my personalities,
But I've never seen you try.

Lead me the way I want to someday lead.
But don't try to force me.
I am no steed.

Write me what's in your head, hold nothing back.
Tell me not of myself;
Tell me what I lack.

Hum my name and make it a melody of your own.
Do not steal or mimic.
Make it mine, an original.

Tell me everything I've ever done to hurt you.
Tell me as a dear friend
So I can see it and become brand new.

Treat me as a lover, enemy, and friend.
For all these things will one day end.

That Girl

I can say I love you, though I love someone else.
"Mr. Personality," the man you made me dream about.
It's not your fault—you're not for me—
But if you cling, I'll have no sympathy.

I don't wanna be the girl you never get over.
Not "the one who got away," I am no four-leaf clover.
But I won't be the one who makes you want to forget the past,
The one your future girlfriends want to attack.
I'd prefer the in-between, gone but not hated:
The one you fondly miss and smile, the one you're glad to have dated.
Most likely, I'll be a sore spot, salt in the open wound.
The pain in your chest, the better left unsaid and gone all too soon.
Please don't hate me. I didn't mean to fall out of love.
Let me go; pray I don't return, like the white dove.
I'm sorry there's nothing left to say.
You'll hopefully read this one day.

The Last Goodbye

The chapter closed. We're both long gone.
I don't know where we went wrong.
Are you a ghost or poltergeist?
Is your love dead or alive with spite?
You weren't that bad, I even thought you were good.
But now that I'm silent, you scream to be understood.
You shout to the few who have to be on your side,
To the ones you formerly tried to undermine.
Yet your complaints all fall deaf,
And at the cap toss, you'll be left.
For our cults and covens didn't invite you,
So your parents will be the last in the pew.
I know I seem salty, but I'm just disappointed
'Cause I hadn't minded you were my first boyfriend.
Though you act two-faced, you seem joyful.
I wish you the best. Please stay hopeful.

Epilogue

Woolen dress, given to me by a friend.
I saved it for my first date,
An evening I couldn't wait for it to end.
Downhill? No, but I was late.

Admiration, something I'd always wanted,
And you had tons to spare,
But only I spoke, and it left me haunted.
On top of my anxieties, it felt unfair.

(That's not your fault. I'm sorry if I made it seem so.
Only the roses were yours to blame. I've made that
known.)

I'm writing you to say I reminisce the end.
Me in the grass, looking at the stars,
Eating the taffy I meant to save for a friend.
We almost froze waiting for our cars.

15. Past Dawn

Time of Night

The sun seeps into the ground.
The bees and ants finish their rounds.
All is quiet, all's asleep,
Yet in my room, I begin to weep.
One cannot cry with the sun in their eyes.
The clock still ticks. Time still flies.

Night's Reign

The sun is gone, and the moon rises. Time stops—
No more minutes, seconds, and hours on old clocks.
Night holds the key to timelessness in her hand,
The secret hundreds have tried to command.
But at midnight in the parking lot or alone in my bed,
I find not slipping spots but portals with no time instead.
Was it hours where we talked without a worry?
Was I in minutes when I didn't have to hurry?
I don't know and maybe never will,
But it was dark past my windowsill.
When all the world's asleep, tucked in Night's arms,
That's where you're safe away from Time's harm.
At midnight or at the first ray of sunshine
Is where we don't have to fall in line.
With those nocturnal, I outrun my pain.
A place without time. I love Night's reign.

Hope

You cannot hide hope away.
It cannot be destroyed;
It cannot be silenced,
It screams into the void.
Try and keep it hidden, it will thrive
And overgrow all.
For hope is all that makes us alive.
An eternal waterfall.

Noon

The inevitable, the terrible,
Will not scare me away.
The bound to become will make some run,
No matter what I say.

Who knew a bluebird or bouquet's word
Would make me feel the same?
A loved one's sudden death and baby's breath
Could both cause me some pain?

Standing below the sun, thinking of someone,
With acorns underfoot.
Knowing that she's not here, you'd disappear.
For you, I might not look.

It's not that I don't care. I do, I swear.
It's just too much, too soon.
I'd rather be alone than checking my phone.
But I'll meet you at noon.

Sources (and a list of poems in written order)

1Clark, Dodie. "In The Middle." *You.* 2017.
https://www.google.com/search?q=in+the+middle+dodie
&rlz=1CAHKDC_enUS883&oq=in&aqs=chrome.0.69i59
j46i39j69i57j69i60l2j69i61j69i65l2.1531j0j4&sourceid=chr
ome&ie=UTF-8

2Boeckmann, Catherine. "Flower Meanings: the
language of flowers." *The Old Farmer's Almanac.*
02/03/2020
https://www.almanac.com/content/flower-meanings-lang
uage-flowers

A Thought from 2018 (2018)   The Color Blue/Love (2018)
Why Can't I? (07.24.20)   3 Weeks (07.27.20)
Tears (08.15.20)
Take Me to the Gardens (10.31.20)
You (11.11.20)   Lost/Known (11.18.20)
A Journey Through a Maze (Nov 2020)
In the Meadows (Nov 2020 1)   Heritage (Nov 2020 2)
A Rainy Week (Nov 2020 3)
In the Clover Field (Nov 2020 4)
No Jackolantern (Nov 2020 5)   Unfathomable (Nov 2020 6)
Escape from Reality (11.30.20)   First Loves (Nov/Dec 2020)
Teachers and Weeds (12.02.20)
Teacher's Blossoms (12.02.20)
Clovers in a Chainlink Fence (12.06.20)
12/07/20 (12/07.20)
A Bouquet of Roses and Baby's Breath (12.07.20)
Past Self (12.11.20)   The Funeral's Echo (12.11.20)
Introduction (12.12.20)   Lost in Fog (12.13.20)

Thoughts From a Sunday (12.13.20)

Broken Toys (12.13.20) — I'm Fine (12.14&15.20)

Downfall (12.16.20) — Maybe (Dec 2020)

Homes (Dec 2020 1) — Noon (Dec 2020 2)

All Good Things ... (12.21.20) — Can You? (12.21.20)

Generation (12.27&28.20) — Song: Villain (12.28.20)

Changes (12.28.20) — Our End (12.28.20)

The Eve Before (12.31.20) — New Year's Day (01.01.21)

A Conversation With a Friend (Jan 2021)

Sunday Morning (Jan 10, 21) — That Girl (01.13.21)

A Prayer (01.16.21) — Anxieties (01.21.21)

Promises (01.24.21) — Epilogue (01.28.21)

Closer and Still (02.08.21) — Poem #12 (02.08.21)

Where You Are (02.10.21) — Masterpiece (02.14.21)

Let Me (02.17.21) — Galaxy Boy (02.22.21)

This Wave Will Crash (02.24.21) — Born to Die (03.01.21)

Accidents (03.03.21) — Golden hour (03.03.21)

Time of Night (03.03.21) — Night's Reign (03.03.21)

Former Friend (03.08.21) — Road of Life (03.10.21)

Muse (03.15.21) — Pleasure (03.17.21)

Peace and War (03.17.21) — Over it (03.22.21)

Summer's tip (03.29.21)

A Joker in a Saint's Skin (03.29.21)

Time to Stop (04.02.21)

The Age of Friendships (04.05.21)

Greek Goddess (04.05.21) — Senior Year (04.12.21)

Our Last Goodbye (04.16.21) — Our Old News (04.16.21)

Role Model (04.19.21) — Mirror (04.21.21)

A Poem for Myself (04.26.21) — Watch Me (05.02.21)

The Storm (05.03.21) — For the Siren (05.03.21)

Hope (05.05.21) — Crashing Down (05.05.21)

UNKNOWN DATE OF ORIGIN:

A Ghost's Lullaby — The Lightning

Crushes	Bathroom Floor
Fleeting Thought	Plague Mask Guy
Maybe Best Friend	

Acknowledgments

Denise Weimer, thank you for helping me edit this. As an overthinker, I am constantly worried about making things perfect and thanks to you I'm not (as) stressed about this book being messy.

To the friends I lost. I want to say I'm sorry for how I reacted, but I'm not sorry for the poems. I hurt *so* much and you didn't acknowledge it, which made it hurt more. I found sanctuary in writing how I felt and I hope you can forgive me for that.

To my kindergarten teacher, my mom, Nanette, Kristy, Rebekah, Paula, and Sheri Michelle. Thank you for making my learning experience brighter. You have no idea how much of an impact you and your class made on my life.

To the teachers who failed me. Thanks for teaching me about procrastination, gaslighting, gatekeeping, and R.B.F. The lessons were valuable and I'm better off for knowing now rather than later.

Thank you, Jamie, Ashlyn, Sophi, Emma, Susan, Hannah, Mae, Tabby, Abby, Caleb, Mitchell, and Lilly for letting me use pictures with you in them for the cover.

About the Author

A.C. "Abby" Ham, an eighteen-year-old artist, recently published her first book, *Justin Strikes: The Unknown Inflictor*. A.C. considers herself to be very artsy, and when she's not writing poems about her feelings, she's doodling abstracts or sketching strangers. A.C. is the oldest of two children and currently resides in the Athens area with her family. A.C. is currently working on continuing the Justin Strikes saga—a gripping series about kids with superpowers trying to find the villain hiding at their school—as well as writing short stories and poems for future compilations.

A.C. on Social Media:

Instagram (for art): cartripcomics
Instagram (for writing): officialjustinstrikes
Facebook: Abby Ham
Youtube: Abby Ham
Tumblr: therealabbyham